COUNTRIES IN OUR WORLD

EGYPT
IN OUR WORLD

Ali Brownlie Bojang

A⁺
Smart Apple Media

Published by Smart Apple Media
P.O. Box 3263, Mankato, Minnesota 56002

Printed in the United States of America at Corporate
Graphics, in North Mankato, Minnesota.

Published by arrangement with the Watts Publishing
Group LTD, London.

Library of Congress Cataloging-in-Publication Data
Brownlie Bojang, Ali, 1949-
  Egypt in our world / by Ali Brownlie Bojang.
    p. cm. -- (Countries in our world)
  Includes bibliographical references and index.
  Summary: "Describes the economy, government, and
culture of Egypt today and discusses Egypt's influence
of and relations with the rest of the world"--Provided
by publisher.
  ISBN 978-1-59920-386-7 (library binding)
  1. Egypt--Juvenile literature. I. Title.
  DT49.B76 2012
  932--dc22

                              2010030845

1305
3-2011

9 8 7 6 5 4 3 2 1

Produced by White-Thompson Publishing Ltd.
Series consultant: Rob Bowden
Editor: Sonya Newland
Designer: Clare Nicholas
Picture researcher: Amy Sparks

Picture Credits
Corbis: 6 (Sandro Vannini), 7 (Bettmann), 9 (Mike
Nelson/epa), 12 (Blaine Harrington III), 17 (Thomas
Hartwell), 19 (Christian Liewig), 22 (Mike Nelson/epa),
25 (Kevin Fleming), 29 (Jose Fuste Raga); **Dreamstime:**
1 (Niek), 5 (Odyssei), 8 (Niek), 10 (Oleg Znamenskiy),
11 (Card76), 13 (Javarman), 16 (Daniel Lesniak), 23
(Richard Carey); **iStock:** 20 (Amanda Lewis); **Getty
Images:** 15, 24 (Time & Life Pictures), 26 (AFP); **Simon
Player:** 14; **Shutterstock:** 18 (Hailin Chen), 28 (Timur
Kulgarin); **UN Photo:** 27 (C. Dufka); **Wikimedia:** 21
(Benjamin Franck).

Contents

▶ Introducing Egypt 4

▶ Landscapes and Environment 8

▶ Population and Migration 12

▶ Culture and Lifestyles 16

▶ Economy and Trade 20

▶ Government and Politics 24

▶ Egypt in 2020 28

▶ Glossary 30

▶ Further Information 31

▶ Index 32

Introducing Egypt

Egypt boasts one of the oldest civilizations in the world, dating back more than 5,000 years. Modern Egypt is an exciting mix of traditional and modern cultures, of rich and poor, and of city and countryside. It is a major player in the politics and trade of both Africa and the Middle East.

IT STARTED HERE

Early Civilization

Egyptian civilization contributed the first organized government to the world. Ancient Egyptians also developed methods of irrigation to help grow their crops, and they used the earliest known alphabet.

Where in the World?

Egypt is one of only three countries in the world (the others are Turkey and Russia) that lie on two continents. It is situated in northeast Africa and on the Sinai Peninsula, which is part of Asia. Although clearly an African country, the Middle Eastern influence is strong in Egypt. As well as its land borders, Egypt is bordered by the Mediterranean Sea in the north and by the Red Sea in the east.

An Ancient Civilization

One of the world's earliest civilizations grew up on the banks of the Nile River in Egypt. The river gave the ancient Egyptians water to grow their crops, and the surrounding desert provided protection against attack from other peoples. For 3,000 years, Egyptian culture flourished. Egyptians built huge pyramids, sphinxes, and statues as tombs and monuments to their rulers, called pharaohs.

▼ *Egypt has land borders with the Gaza Strip and Israel to the northeast, Sudan to the south, and Libya to the west.*

Influences and Occupations

Beginning in 341 BC, Egypt was ruled by a series of invaders from Persia (now Iran), Greece, and Rome. In the seventh century, the Arabs came to Egypt and introduced the Islamic religion and the Arabic language. The Arabs ruled Egypt for the next 600 years until the Turks conquered them in 1517 and took control of Egypt.

IT'S A FACT!

The Great Pyramid of Giza is the only one of the Seven Wonders of the Ancient World that is still standing. It is 482 feet (147 m) tall and was the tallest monument in the world until the nineteenth century.

▼ *In the desert outside Cairo stand the Sphinx and the Great Pyramid of Giza— remains of the ancient Egyptian civilization.*

The Suez Canal

During the 19th century, both France and Britain took an interest in Egypt. They helped to pay for the building of the Suez Canal in 1869. This created a 100-mile (163 km) shortcut from Europe to India and the rest of Asia. Ships no longer had to go all the way around Africa. This was very important to countries like Britain that were trying to increase their influence over world trade. In 1882, Britain seized control of the Egyptian government to safeguard its interest in the Suez Canal. For the next 70 years Britain had some control over Egypt, although there was still an Egyptian king and an Egyptian prime minister and parliament.

GOING GLOBAL

The Suez Canal is an important trade route. In 2008, an average of 1,780 ships passed through in a month. Between 2000 and 2008, the amount of shipping from Southeast Asia and the Far East, including China, passing through the canal increased by two-and-a-half times. This shows how important the Suez Canal has been for Chinese exports to Europe.

▼ *A container ship passes through the Suez Canal. Fourteen percent of total world trade and 26 percent of world oil exports travel via this waterway.*

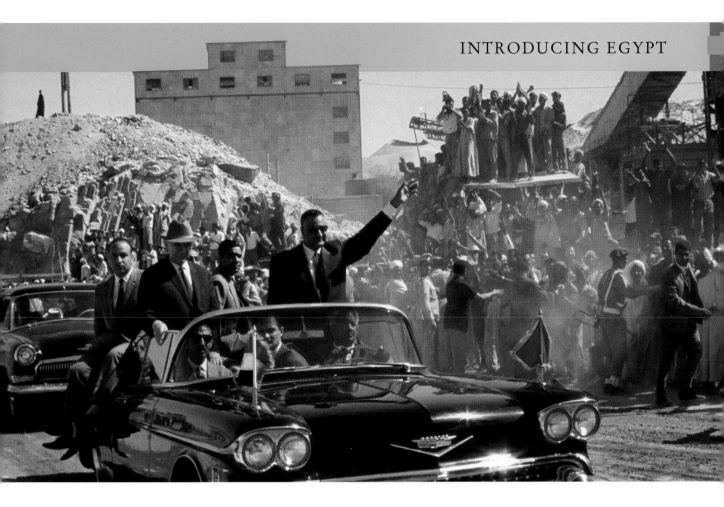

The Egyptian Republic

In 1952, a group of soldiers led by Gamal Abdel Nasser staged a revolution. They intended to overthrow the king, Farouk, who they thought was corrupt and too influenced by the British. The revolution was a success and the monarchy was abolished. In 1953, the new Egyptian republic was born.

▲ *Gamal Abdel Nasser (waving), leader of the revolution and second president of Egypt, drives through the streets of Cairo.*

Egypt's Place in the World

Egypt is still a major channel for international trade. The country's role as a go-between and mediator in the Middle East is also becoming more important, as problems between its neighbors, Israel and Palestine, worsen. Egypt has a good relationship with the United States—which it supported during the Gulf War in 1990—and the European Union (EU), as well as being a key player in the Arab world.

BASIC DATA

Official name:	**Arab Republic of Egypt**
Capital:	**Cairo**
Size:	**386,662 sq miles (1,001,450 sq km)**
Population:	**80,471,869 (2010 est.)**
Currency:	**Egyptian pound**

Landscapes and Environment

Egypt is a plateau made up of sand and rock. Across this dry landscape flows the longest river in the world, the Nile, and on either side of the river are fertile valleys. The Nile is the lifeline of Egypt, providing water for drinking and crops.

The Nile River

The Nile flows for 960 miles (1,545 km) through Egypt, creating a green line through the desert. In the past, the river would flood every year and leave behind a fine fertile silt. This created an area up to 7.5 miles (12 km) on either side of the river where farming could take place. With the help of irrigation, people were able to grow a wide variety of crops, such as cotton, rice, corn, wheat, beans, fruit, and other vegetables. They raised cattle, water buffalo, sheep, and goats. Today, any flooding of the Nile is controlled by the Aswan High Dam.

IT'S A FACT!

The Nile Delta, where the river spreads out and flows into the Mediterranean Sea, is one of the largest deltas in the world. It covers 150 miles (240 km) of the Mediterranean coastline and is about 100 miles (160 km) in length from north to south. The Nile Delta is the winter home of some of the largest groups of birds in the world, including little gulls and whiskered terns.

▼ *Traditional Egyptian boats, called* feluccas, *sailing on the Nile.*

Climate

Egypt is hot and dry with very little rainfall. The capital, Cairo, receives no more than 0.4 inches (10 mm) of rain a year, which usually falls in the cool season between December and February. Farther south, the amount of rainfall decreases even more. In some desert locations it may rain only once every few years. During April, dust storms are common, caused by the hot Sirocco wind that blows from the Sahara Desert.

▲ *Tourists protect their faces from the sand and dust in Cairo.*

PLACE IN THE WORLD

Total area: **386,662 sq miles (1,001,450 sq km)**

Percentage of world land area: **0.67%**

World ranking: **30th**

The Deserts

About 95 percent of Egypt is desert. In this harsh environment where temperatures can reach over 122°F (50°C), very few plants, animals, or people can survive. The Western Desert, which is actually part of the Sahara Desert, is the largest desert in the world. This is a relatively flat area, covering about two-thirds of the country. Strong winds have

▲ In Egypt's deserts, the wind creates limestone rock formations and high sand dunes.

blown the sand into dunes more than 100 feet (30 m) high—as tall as a 10-story building. Here, the wind also forms large limestone rock formations. To the east of the country lie the more rocky and mountainous Eastern and Sinai deserts.

Highs and Lows

The highest point in Egypt is Mount Catherine, which lies towards the southern tip of the Sinai Peninsula and is 8,625 feet (2,629 m) high. Mountainous peaks running down the coast of the Red Sea reach 2,461 feet (750 m). In the Western Desert there are vast low-lying hollows. The largest of these is the Qattara Depression, a huge area of salt pans and rocks. At 436 feet (133 m) below sea level, this is the second-lowest point in Africa.

Environmental Problems

Egypt's exceptionally dry climate and its large population create huge demands for water and fertile land. Vital farmland is being taken over by the growing cities, and in some places, lost to the deserts. To produce more food from less land, farmers use more fertilizers and pesticides on their crops. These pollute the Nile River, adding to the pollution from sewage and waste from the cities. The Red Sea, with its coral reefs, is also threatened by oil pollution and increasing tourism.

IT'S A FACT!

Global warming is causing sea levels to rise, threatening Egypt's low-lying but densely populated delta area and the ability to grow crops there, as well as destroying many of its ancient structures. Scientists predict that by 2020, more than 15 percent of the valuable delta area will have been lost. Egypt serves as a warning to other countries about what may happen if climate-change issues are not addressed.

▼ *This area of the Nile Delta could be flooded in a few decades as a result of global warming.*

Egypt's population of approximately 80 million is the largest of any Arab-speaking country and the second largest in Africa after Nigeria. Most of Egypt's rapidly increasing population lives on the small strip of land around the Nile River.

Who are the Egyptians?

Egypt's inhabitants are a mix of races, descended from the ancient Egyptians, Berbers from other parts of North Africa, and sub-Saharan Africans such as the Nubians. There are also groups descended from the Arabs, Greeks, and Turks. Most Egyptians live along the fertile banks of the Nile River and in its delta. There are small communities of people in the oases of the Western Desert and in the oil-drilling and mining towns of the Arabian Desert.

PLACE IN THE WORLD

Population: **80,471,869 (2010 est.)**

Percentage of world total: **1.18%**

World ranking: **16th**

▼ *Nubia covers part of southern Egypt and stretches into northern Sudan. Here, a Nubian woman collects water from a canal running through her village near Aswan.*

City Living

Over 40 percent of the population lives in cities such as Cairo, Alexandria, Subra al-Haymah, and Luxor. Egypt's cities have grown quickly. In 1850, the population of Cairo was 250,000. Today it is around 17 million, and it is the largest city in Africa. The populations of the cities swell daily as people commute to work from the towns and villages nearby.

Population Density

About 95 percent of Egyptians live along the Nile, which is about five percent of the total land area. This concentration has created one of the most densely populated areas in the world. On average, there are 3,980 people per square mile (1,535 per sq km) along the Nile. In comparison, the density in all of Egypt is 209 people per square mile (81 per sq km).

IT'S A FACT!

In the deserts of Egypt live small groups of people called Bedouins. Although they are divided into different tribes, they have several similar customs and are known for their folk music and dance. In the past, Bedouins were nomadic—they moved around throughout the year. Today many of them live in permanent settlements in desert areas, and some have also now settled in Egypt's large cities.

▼ *Alexandria is the second largest city in Egypt with a population of more than 4 million.*

Population Growth

Egypt's population has grown very rapidly in recent years. It more than doubled between 1970 and 2000. Although the rate at which it is growing has now slowed down, it is still increasing by about 1.5 million people every year. One-third of Egyptians are under 14 years old, and in the near future they will be looking for work, houses, and healthcare, as well as schools for their own children.

Finding Jobs

Job opportunities in Egypt are scarce and salaries are low. Many Egyptians leave the country to find work and higher wages in Saudi Arabia and other countries in the Middle East, Libya, the United States, or Europe. In 2009, it was estimated that 3 million Egyptians were working in other countries. Some of these people are highly educated, working in jobs such as engineering and teaching.

▼ *Although life expectancy at birth is quite high (72.2 years), Egypt has an extremely young population. Only 4.4 percent of the population are over 65.*

Desperate to Leave

As for the Egyptians who have little education and few skills, in their desperation to improve their lives, they cross the Mediterranean Sea to Europe on makeshift boats. It is a dangerous journey, and some die on the way when their boats sink. Some people travel to Egypt especially to make this boat journey. Illegal immigration like this has risen over the past 10 years, but it is impossible to know how many people have successfully reached and settled in Europe. Some experts think it may be as many as 20,000 people a year.

GOING GLOBAL

The money that Egyptians living abroad send home is very important to their families and to Egypt as a whole. In 2007, Egyptians sent home nearly US$6 billion, which has helped the Egyptian economy.

▼ *Illegal immigrants from Egypt and other countries in North Africa arrive in Italy.*

Culture and Lifestyles

Egyptian culture is a mix of the old and the new. It has absorbed ideas and traditions from its invaders and visitors over thousands of years, and combined these with its own ancient traditions.

Religion

The Arabs introduced Islam to Egypt in the seventh century. Today, times of business meetings, films, and concerts are decided by the sound of the call to prayer from the minarets broadcasting system five times a day. Ninety percent of Egyptians are Muslim. In recent years some Egyptians have started to support a stricter form of Islam. More and more women are covering their heads and faces with a veil, or *hijab*. Most other people—around nine percent—are Coptic (Egyptian) Christians, making up the largest Christian population in the Middle East.

▶ *A mosque in the city of Hurghada on the Red Sea coast. This mosque is quite modern—built around 30 years ago—but Islam has been the main religion here since the seventh century.*

Family and Food

Family is important to all Egyptians, although today Egyptian families are getting smaller, as people are choosing to have fewer children. Food is an important part of the hospitality shown to visitors in Egypt. Typical dishes are made from beans and lentils, rice and flatbreads, and vegetables cooked in onions and tomatoes. Egyptian food is similar to that in neighboring countries such as Greece, Lebanon, and Turkey. In the cities, however, wealthy Egyptians frequently eat European food. French cuisine and Western fast food are particularly popular.

IT'S A FACT!

All Egyptian children must attend school between the ages of six and 14. Education is free in government-run schools, although there are private schools available for the children of wealthier Egyptians. Arabic is the official language in Egypt, but many schools also teach French and English.

▼ *Western fast food is popular in large cities. This sign for McDonald's is written in both English and Arabic, Egypt's official language.*

GOING GLOBAL

Many ancient Egyptian objects, such as statues and mummies, can be found in museums all over the world. Some of the best examples are in the British Museum in London, the New York Metropolitan Museum of Art, and the Louvre in Paris. Touring exhibits, such as those displaying the treasures of the pharaoh Tutankhamen, have been sell-outs in countries such as the United States and United Kingdom.

▲ *This obelisk, known as Cleopatra's Needle, once guarded an ancient temple at Luxor. Now it stands in Paris's Place de la Concorde.*

Life in the Country

Country life in Egypt is very different from life in the cities. In the Nile Delta, for example, there are still peasant farmers, called *fellahins*, wearing the traditional baggy trousers. Most people in rural areas are very poor.

Life in the Cities

In contrast, life in the cities is similar to that in cities all over the United States and Europe. Busy urban areas such as Cairo and Alexandria are packed with people. There are traffic jams and blaring horns, amongst the many office buildings, shopping malls, and restaurants. Despite these signs of Western life, however, only a few of Egypt's city dwellers are as wealthy as Americans or Europeans, and standards of living in Egypt are much lower.

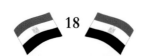

Music

Traditional music in Egypt has been influenced by Arabic music from Persia and India. Its tones and rhythms are very different from Western music. This music is usually played at weddings and festivals. Young Egyptians prefer pop music, and there are many modern pop singers in Egypt today, such as Mohamed Mounir and Amr Diab. Many of these singers base their music on the traditional forms.

THE HOME OF...

Arabic Films

Egypt has been nicknamed the "Hollywood of the Arab world," and is the major supplier of films in this region, producing around 40 a year. An international film festival is held every year in Cairo, and this has gained renown not just among Arab countries, but also those in the Western world.

Sports

Soccer is the most popular sport in Egypt, both for playing and watching. Egyptian soccer clubs, especially El Ahly and El Zamalek, are known throughout the Middle East and Africa. The national team is popularly known as the Pharaohs, and it is the most successful African soccer team, having won the African Nations Cup six times. Other popular sports in Egypt are basketball, handball, squash, and tennis. Egyptian runners are also admired all over the world for their speed and stamina.

▼ *Egypt's national soccer team celebrates winning the African Nations Cup in 2008 after the final against Cameroon.*

Economy and Trade

Only five percent of Egypt's land can be used to grow crops, but 32 percent of the population is involved in farming. The activities that bring in the most foreign money to Egypt are the production and exportation of oil, as well as tourism, money sent home from Egyptians working abroad, and fees from shipping companies using the Suez Canal.

Natural Resources

Oil is Egypt's most valuable natural resource, and in the 1990s Egypt also began exporting natural gas. Both of these are mined near the Red Sea, on the Sinai Peninsula, and in the Western Desert. Phosphate rock (used to make fertilizer), iron ore, and salt are also mined in Egypt. Egypt is self-sufficient in energy, which means it does not rely on other countries for its energy needs. As well as oil, Egypt generates hydroelectricity using the enormous Aswan High Dam. The dam is used to control the Nile floods. However, it also stops some of the silt from being carried down the river, which means the soil in some areas is not as fertile as it used to be.

▼ *The Aswan High Dam provides around 20 percent of Egypt's electricity, but it has caused concern because of the effect it has had on the quality of soil downriver.*

Farming

Nearly all farms in Egypt are located in the Nile Valley and Delta. Traditional farms are small and are irrigated with water from the Nile. On larger, more commercial farms, the land is worked more intensively and fertilizers are used to get the most crops possible. There are usually two crops a year and the main cash crop—crops grown especially for export rather than for personal use—is cotton. Some desert land is being developed for farming, but these systems are very expensive. Water has to be transported by pipes from the Nile, or very deep holes have to be dug to reach underground water supplies.

Trade

Egypt buys more from other countries than it sells to them, which is one reason why Egypt is in debt. Egypt exports oil, ready-made clothes, cotton, and other farming products such as citrus fruit and rice. It sells these mainly to the United States and Italy. Egypt buys food, machinery, and transportation equipment mainly from China, France, Germany, Italy, and the United States.

▶ *Workers in a t-shirt factory. Clothes are big business in Egypt because of the high-quality cotton that can be grown there.*

GLOBAL LEADER

Egyptian Cotton

Egyptian cotton is considered to be the best in the world. It is used to produce high-quality sheets for top department stores and clothes for many well-known high-end shops. However, it is estimated that about a million children in Egypt are employed to help with the cotton harvest, often working in very bad conditions.

Industry

Egypt has manufacturing industries in cities such as Cairo and Alexandria. These produce mainly iron and steel, textiles, plastics, and cars. There are also several oil refineries. Some international companies, such as car manufacturers, have been attracted to Egypt because it has such a large population. This not only provides buyers for the manufactured goods, but also workers who can be paid lower wages than what the companies would pay for labor in their own countries.

Small Businesses

Small businesses can be found in many of Egypt's cities. People repair household items or cars, and recycle metal, litter, and fabrics. They may sell many different products either in small shops or in market stalls. Many of these businesses are not registered and owners do not pay their taxes. It is impossible to know how many people work in this informal way, but the number has been estimated at 7 million.

GLOBAL LEADER

Mubarak Pumping Station
The Mubarak Pumping Station is the largest in the world. It pumps water from Lake Nasser to the Toshka Depression, a large low-lying area of desert. The pump facility is 100 feet (30 m) wide, 460 feet (140 m) long, and 197 feet (60 m) high. It was built in a pit around 15 stories deep, and is 10 times the size of a football stadium.

▼ *In the markets of Egypt, vendors sell locally-made handicrafts such as textiles and objects crafted from metal.*

▲ *The clear, warm water and the variety of fish and coral reefs of the Red Sea offer some of the best scuba diving in the world.*

THE HOME OF...

Scuba Diving

The year-round high temperatures, low rainfall, warm seas, and beautiful coral reefs have enabled the Red Sea town of Sharm el-Sheikh to develop from a small fishing village into one of the world's top scuba-diving resorts.

Tourism

With its good weather, fascinating history, monuments and its beautiful Red Sea resorts such as Sharm-el-Sheikh and Dahab, Egypt is one of the world's top tourist destinations. Tourism is a vital source of foreign income for the country's economy. In 2007, more than 10 million tourists visited Egypt and contributed 11 percent to Egypt's total income, or gross domestic product (GDP). The largest numbers of tourists come from Italy, followed by visitors from Germany and the United Kingdom. The Egyptian government is concerned that fewer tourists may visit Egypt in the coming years because of the bad state of the global economy.

Since independence in 1953, Egypt was ruled by a president and prime minister. In 2011, the people of Egypt staged a protest to have the president step down. After 18 days, Hosni Mubarak resigned, and the military took temporary control of the government.

Transition

During the transition, the military government is working to amend the country's constitution to ensure the people of Egypt have more rights. They have called for fair and democratic elections to take place.

▼ *Egyptian soldiers set off to support U.S. troops during the First Gulf War in 1990.*

Powerful Presidents

In 1953, when Egypt became independent, General Muhammad Naguib, a leader in the revolution, became president. In 1956, another revolution leader, Gamal Abdel Nasser, became president. Nassar was very powerful and wanted to unite all the Arab nations under Egyptian control, so he turned to the USSR for help. This did not please countries in the West, because they were not on good terms with the USSR.

Al-Sadat and Mubarak

The next president, Anwar al-Sadat, distanced Egypt from the USSR and tried to make peace with Israel. This angered some Egyptians and he was assassinated in 1981. Hosni Mubarak was appointed president in 1981 and worked hard to build Egypt's strength in the Arab world and develop good relations with the West.

FAMOUS EGYPTIAN

Anwar al-Sadat (1918–81)

In 1978, President Anwar al-Sadat received the Nobel Peace Prize for his role in improving relations between Egypt and Israel, which he shared with the Israeli prime minister, Menachem Begin. However, in 1981 he was killed by assassins from secret groups who wanted to make Egypt a pure Islamic society and who felt he had betrayed Egypt and Islam.

▼ *Anwar al-Sadat (with sash), shortly before he was assassinated. Mubarak is on the right.*

Human Rights

Several international human rights organizations, such as Amnesty International and Human Rights Watch, have criticized Egypt's record on human rights. People who disagree with the president have been put in jail and tortured. Women do not have the same rights as men, particularly when it comes to marriage and divorce. More and more women in Egypt are calling for equal rights with men, and are starting to take a more active part in politics.

Uprising

In recent years, the government had created constitutional amendments that further limited the rights of Egyptians. In January 2011, the people of Egypt started peaceful protests in Cairo and other major cities. They demanded that President Mubarak resign and that a new constitution ensuring democracy be drafted. During the transition to a democracy, people around the world wait to see what impact the new government will have on relationships with other countries.

▼ *Egyptian journalist Yomna Mokhtar used the social networking site Facebook to campaign for rights for unmarried women, who are regarded as inferior in Egypt.*

International Links

Egypt is a member of several influential international organizations, including the Arab League, the African Union, and the United Nations. Membership of these groups has allowed Egypt to have a say about many international issues, and to play a significant role in world events such as trade agreements and peacekeeping missions in troubled countries.

▼ *Boutros Boutros-Ghali (left) on a visit to Rwanda during his time as Secretary-General of the United Nations.*

FAMOUS EGYPTIAN

Boutros Boutros-Ghali (b. 1922)

Boutros Boutros-Ghali was born in Cairo in 1922. He was an Egyptian diplomat and became the sixth Secretary-General of the United Nations, holding this position from January 1992 to January 1997. During his time as Secretary-General, he had to deal with issues such as the Rwandan genocide, the Angolan Civil War, and the wars in the former Yugoslavia.

Egypt in 2020

One of the biggest challenges Egypt faces is the need for land and water to provide for its growing population. This issue could be made more difficult by the threat of climate change.

The Need for Land

As the overcrowded cities of Egypt continue to expand, they will take up valuable farming land. To solve this problem, the government has started some major projects to develop the deserts. By 2017, it estimates that it will have converted 3.5 million acres (1.5 million ha) of desert into productive farmland. Water for these projects is provided by deep wells that tap into a huge water reserve beneath the Sahara Desert.

▲ *As Egypt's population continues to grow, slums are springing up on the outskirts of the cities. Providing adequate housing is a priority for the Egyptian government.*

The Need for Water

As Egypt's population grows there will be a greater need for water for homes, for crops, for factories, and to create power. One big concern is what countries upriver on the Nile do to affect the waters. As they take more

water to fulfill their own needs, for example, it may decrease the amount of water available to the Egyptians. Although there is an agreement in place about water use, some experts think tension over water could lead to the world's first "water war."

Climate Change

Climate change, along with the rise in sea levels, is a major threat to the food-producing Nile Delta region. Scientists have predicted that the Mediterranean will rise between 12 inches (30 cm) and 3 feet (1 m) by the end of the twenty-first century. This would flood coastal areas along the Delta.

Developing a Modern Country

For thousands of years, Egypt has faced the limitations of its deserts and climate. By and beyond 2020 it will continue to face these and other challenges. However, its already strong influence, particularly in the Middle East, is likely to develop further in the near future, helping Egypt become an even more important player on the world stage.

▼ *Dealing with the dry climate is one of Egypt's biggest challenges, but ancient treasures such as the pyramids and great temples will continue to attract tourists and boost the economy.*

Glossary

Arab someone who belongs to a race of people that originated in the Arabian Peninsula.

cash crops crops that are grown especially to be exported to other countries.

Christianity a religion that follows the teachings of Jesus Christ.

coral reefs underwater structures formed from the remains of sea creatures.

economy the financial system of a country or region, including how much money is made from the production and sale of goods and services.

export to transport products or materials abroad for sale or trade.

feluccas traditional Egyptian sailing boats with flat bottoms and triangular sails.

global warming the gradual rise in temperature on the surface of the earth, caused by changes in the amount of greenhouse gases in the atmosphere.

gross domestic product (GDP) the total amount of money a country earns every year.

immigrant a person who has moved to another country to live.

irrigation supplying dry land with water by means of ditches and channels.

Islam a religion with belief in one god (Allah) and his last prophet, Muhammad.

Muslim a follower of the Islamic religion.

nomadic moving from place to place, often to find the best grazing land for herds of livestock.

oasis a fertile or green area in a desert where there is a source of water.

plateau an area of high, flat land.

pollution harmful materials that damage the air, water, and soil, such as vehicle emissions, waste gases from factories, or chemicals from fertilizers.

population density the number of people living in a square mile or square kilometer of a country.

pyramids large structures built as tombs for the ancient Egyptian pharaohs.

republic a form of government in which a country is ruled not by a king or queen, but by officials elected by the people.

rural relating to the countryside.

salt pans small, undrained, shallow depressions where water builds up and evaporates, leaving salt behind.

silt fine particles of earth deposited by rivers.

Further Information

Books

Visit Egypt!
Crabtree Connections
by Jill Laidlaw
(Crabtree Pub, 2010)

Egypt
QEB Travel Through
by Elaine Jackson
(QEB Publishing, 2008)

Welcome to Egypt
Welcome to the World
by Patrick Ryan
(Child's World, 2008)

Focus on Egypt
World in Focus
by Jen Green
(World Almanac Library, 2007)

Egypt
A True Book
by Howard Gutner
(Children's Press, 2009)

Egypt
Destination Detectives
by Nicola Barber
(Raintree, 2006)

Web Sites

http://www.touregypt.net/Kids/
A site for children offering a virtual tour of Egypt, with information about its history and monuments as well as games and activities.

http://www.horus.ics.org.eg/en/Default_HTML.aspx
The Little Horus website, where readers are guided through information on Egypt by the sky god.

https://www.cia.gov/library/publications/the-world-factbook/geos/eg.html
The CIA World Factbook entry on Egypt gives statistics and information on the land, people, government, and economy of Egypt.

http://travel.nationalgeographic.com/travel/countries/egypt-guide
A guide to Egypt with articles, photos, facts, videos, and news from National Geographic

Every effort has been made by the publisher to ensure that these web sites contain no inappropriate or offensive material. However, because of the nature of the Internet, it is impossible to guarantee that the content of these sites will not be altered. We strongly advise that Internet access is supervised by a responsible adult.

Index

Numbers in **bold** indicate pictures

A
Africa 4, 6, 19
African Union 27
Alexandria 13, **13**, 18, 22
Al-Sadat, Anwar 25, **25**
Arab League 27
armed forces 24, **24**
Asia 4, 6
Aswan High Dam 8, 20, **20**
B
Bedouins 13
Boutros-Ghali, Boutros 27, **27**
C
Cairo 9, **9**, 13, 18, 19, 22, 27
Catherine, Mount 11
China 6, 21
climate 9, 11, 23, 29
climate change 11, 28, 29
coral reefs 11, 23, **23**
cotton 8, 21
crops 4, 8, 11, 20, 21, 28
D
Dahab 23
deserts 9, 10, **10**, 11, 12, 13, 20,
  21, 28, 29
Diab, Amr 19
dust storms 9, **9**
E
economy 15, 23
education 14, 15, 17
environmental issues 11, 29
Europe 6, 14, 15, 17, 18
exports 20, 21

F
family 17
farming 8, 11, 20, 21, 28
Farouk, King 7
food 17, **17**
France 6, 21
G
Germany 21, 23
Giza 5, **5**
government 4, 6, 17, 24–27, 28
H
human rights 26
hydroelectricity 20
I
immigrants 15, **15**
irrigation 4, 8, 21
Israel 7, 25, 26
Italy **15**, 21, 23
L
language 5, 17
Luxor 13
M
markets 22, **22**
Mediterranean Sea 4, 8, 15, 29
Middle East 4, 14, 16, 19, 29
Mounir, Mohammed 19
Mubarak, Hosni 24–25, **25**, 27
Mubarak Pumping Station 22
music 13, 19
N
Nasser, Gamal Abdel 7, **7**, 25
Nile Delta 8, **10-11**, 11, 12, 18,
  21, 29

Nile River 4, 8, **8**, 12, 13, 20, 21, 28
Nubians 12, **12**
O
oil 20, 21, 22
P
pharaohs 5, 18
pollution 11
population 11, 12, 13, 14, 20, 22
president 24, 25, 26
prime minister 6, 24
pyramids 5, **5**, 23
R
Red Sea 4, 11, 20, 23, **23**
religion 4, 5, 16, 25
S
scuba diving 23, **23**
Sharm el-Sheikh 23
Sinai Peninsula 4, 11, 20
sports 19, **19**
Subra al-Haymah 13
Suez Canal 6, **6**, 20
T
temples 23, **29**
tourism 11, 20, 23
trade 4, 6, 7, 21, 27
Turkey 4, 17
Tutankhamen 18
U
United Kingdom 13, 18, 23
United Nations 27, **27**
United States 7, 14, 18, 21
W
water 11, 28, 29